·Brownie·

·Year·Book·

Copyrighted by Palmer Cox.

CHARLES E. TUTTLE COMPANY
Rutland · Vermont & Tokyo · Japan

REPRESENTATIVES

British Isles & Continental Europe:
SIMON & SCHUSTER INTERNATIONAL GROUP, London
Australasia: BOOKWISE INTERNATIONAL
1 Jeanes Street, Beverley, 5009, South Australia

Published by the Charles E. Tuttle Company, Inc.
of Rutland, Vermont & Tokyo, Japan
with editorial offices at
Suido 1-chome, 2-6, Bunkyo-ku, Tokyo

© 1988 by Charles E. Tuttle Company

Library of Congress Catalog Card No. 87-51207
International Standard Book No. 0-8048-1553-4

First published by McLoughlin Bros., New York, 1895
First Tuttle edition, 1988

Printed in Japan

PUBLISHER'S FOREWORD

"It is doubtful" wrote *The New York Times*, "whether any fashion in children's literature has ever swept a country so completely as when Palmer Cox's Brownies took possession of American childhood in the early eighties."

Amazingly, this comment was written almost a hundred years ago, for the charm and character of these illustrated stories and verses has hardly dimmed with the passing of time. This delightful new facsimile edition of the *Brownie Year Book* is certain to find a new and enthusiastic readership, both among children coming to them for the first time, and those in whom they rekindle memories of their own youth.

It was not until he was forty years old that Palmer Cox (1840–1924) began illustrating the stories in the children's magazine, *St. Nicholas*, that were to become the famous Brownie series. Inspired by legends Cox had heard as a child in Canada from the emigrant Scots, the Brownies were modified to fit the environment of the nineteenth-century American child. So successfully was this achieved, that they brought joy and entertainment to a whole generation, and over a million copies of the thirteen Brownie books were sold within Palmer Cox's lifetime.

In his books, Cox "organizes" his Brownies, sending them out to do good in the world. He resolved that there should be no pain or crime in the beings of his creation, only laughter for children. They, in turn, responded to his ideas. Each character in the series was unmistakably drawn, and was easily recognizable. Thus children could, and invariably did, identify each of the characters with someone they knew in real life, and follow them through the various adventures. In the *Brownie Year Book*, this is as true today as when it was first published in 1895.

.JANUARY.

Throughout the year the Brownie Band
For pleasure travels o'er the land:
In January, when the snow
Lies on the hills and valleys low,
And from the north the chilly breeze
Comes whistling through the naked trees,
Upon toboggans long they ride
For hours down the mountain side,
Until the broadening light of day
Compels them all to quit their play.

. FEBRUARY .

When ice has coated lake and stream,
And skating is the common theme
Of which the youthful people speak
By night and day from week to week;
The Brownies are not left behind
But manage well their sport to find,
And keep it up till ice grows thin
And daring skaters tumble in;
Thus February brings delight
To cunning Brownies every night.

When March arrives with sweeping gales
That bend the trees and split the sails,
And people have a lively chase
For hats that will not keep their place,
Then to the field the Brownies bring
Their home-made kites and balls of string;
And there for hours they run about,
Now holding down now letting out,
And shouting as they see them rise
Like birds when soaring to the skies.

PALMER COX

·APRIL·

When fall the drenching April showers
To start the grass and bud the flowers,
Each cunning Brownie must be spry
To keep his scanty garments dry;
For they know where in wood or field
The friendly tree will shelter yield,
And if the place should prove too small
To safely hide or house them all,
The Brownies with a ready mind
Will turn to use whate'er they find.

·MAY·

When flowers spring on every side,
In gardens fair, and meadows wide,
The Brownies quickly take the chance
That's offered for a merry dance.
They place the tapering pole upright
To which they fasten ribbons bright,
Then two and two they run and play
And wind the ribbons as they may;
Until across the dewy lawn
They catch the hint of coming dawn.

·JUNE·

In sunny June when skies are bright,
And woods and water do invite
The people from their tasks away
To sport themselves by night and day,
The Brownies are not slow to take
A ride upon a pleasant lake,
Or follow fast by rock and tree
A stream that hastens to the sea;
Though dangers may the band surround
Before the night has circled round.

·JULY·

When July has its visits paid,
And trees afford a grateful shade,
And stretched across from tree to tree
The hammocks swing above the lea,
The Brownies are not slow to find
Where people through the day reclined;
And climbing in with laugh and shout
They load it down till strands give out,
And then confusion does surprise
Each Brownie that beneath it lies.

AUGUST.

To swim and sport in August mild
Though water may be calm or wild,
Gives pleasure to the Brownie Band
Who haste at night to reach the strand,
That they may plunge into the wave
To swim and dive, or like a stave,
To float on water, to and fro,
Without a stir of hand or toe,
And strive each other to outdo
By wond'rous skill and methods new..

·SEPTEMBER·

When fish in lake and river bright
At tempting bait are prone to bite,
And people from the rock or boat,
Watch bobbing corks that drifting float;
The Brownies also take delight,
And spend the mild September night
In landing fish of every kind
That is awake and well inclined
To seize the bait that's dropped below,
With all the skill the Brownies know.

. OCTOBER .

When woods are tinged with all the glow
October on the woods can throw,
And game is plenty on the tree
And every kind of weapon free;
The Brownies imitate the way
Mankind does creep upon the prey;
And hiding by each rock and hill
Move up and down with caution still,
And only stop the sport on hand
When morning smiles upon the land.

·NOVEMBER·

November's winds are keen and cold,
As Brownies know who roam the wold
And have no home to which to run
When they have had their night of fun,
But cunning hands are never slow
To build a fire of ruddy glow
Where they can sit and toast their toes
And warm each finger tip that shows
A sign of frost, that brings despair
To those who have no gloves to wear.

When comes the month that calls to mind
The day so dear to all mankind,
The people living West or East,
Begin to talk about the feast
That will be spread for young and old,
While songs are sung and stories told.
December does no less awake
The thoughts of pudding or of cake
In every Brownie in the band,
Who well such dainties understand.